Learning to Live Lightly

JANE HOLMES

Dear Jenny,

May you always walk in the light of Jesus!

Jane Holmes

Learning to Live Lightly
Copyright © 2020 by Jane Holmes.

All rights reserved. No part of this publication may be reproduced, distributed, or transmitted in any form or by any means, including photocopying, recording, or other electronic or mechanical methods, without the prior written permission of the publisher, except in the case of brief quotations embodied in critical reviews and certain other noncommercial uses permitted by copyright law. For permission requests, write to the author at mrswtjj2002@gmail.com.

Unless otherwise noted, Scripture quotations marked (NKJV) are taken from the New King James Version®. Copyright © 1982 by Thomas Nelson. Used by permission. All rights reserved.

Proofreading and typesetting: Sally Hanan of Inksnatcher.com

Cover design: www.fiverr.com/germancreative

Special discounts are available on quantity purchases by corporations, associations, churches, and others. For details, contact the author at the email address above.

Learning to Live Lightly/Jane Holmes
ISBN 978-1-7773255-0-3

I dedicate this book to my family and all my friends who have accompanied me on this journey, however briefly, over the years. Each one has contributed to my gratitude for the many and various encounters along the way and made an impact on my life.

Above all, I dedicate my humble effort as a sacrifice of praise to Jesus Christ my Lord, who is the Light of the World.

Contents

Introduction vii

1. Loss of a Spouse 1
2. Walking in the Dark 15
3. Riding in the Rain 21
4. Hiding in the Dark 25
5. It's about Your Health 33
6. Health Education 39
7. My Own Family 45
8. Boundaries 51
9. Stepping Up, Speaking Up 61
10. Darby and the Soup Kitchen 71
11. A Place in the Country 81
12. Mind, Body, and Spirit 89

Conclusion 95

About the Author 97
Health Leaders 99

Introduction

WE ARE OFTEN weighed down by the world and its grievances. Whether we face natural disasters or personal hardships, life impacts our sense of well-being and outlook. When darkness weighs heavily upon our body, mind, or spirit, we must learn to live lightly.

Seventy-odd years qualifies me to speak from experience with just a few instances that reflect my walk of faith and of learning to trust in the Lord and to rely on His promises.

The benefits of trusting God will always outweigh the hardships and the heaviness. He came to redeem the whole human race, and He has given clear evidence of His love and power in His life, death, and resurrection. He has been faithful through all generations. He will be faithful to you as you trust Him.

Do not ignore or bypass the opportunity to seek Him. Make the decision to trust in His everlasting love and power to save you, in this world and for eternity. By placing your heart in the Saviour's hands, you will be learning to live lightly.

Jane Holmes

Loss of a Spouse

— 1 —

Life vs Death

I MARRIED MY AMAZING FRIEND at the age of twenty-one. He was four years older than I and lived only a few miles away. Oddly enough, we didn't meet until I was nineteen. My brother, who had become friends with him, introduced us. A township line divided our communities, so we had attended different schools, and our paths hadn't crossed until then.

The first time we met, my brother was giving me a ride home to our farm from the city. At a local stop sign, a car pulled alongside ours and stopped because the guys in the car knew my brother.

"Where are you going, and who is the chick with you?" asked one of the guys, Bill. He was referring to me.

My brother answered, "Oh, this is my sister. Just giving her a ride home."

Bill continued, "We're all going to the Pow Wow for something to eat. Want to come?" My brother looked at me and asked me if I wanted to go. I looked at him, raising my eyebrows. Was he kidding? Of course I wanted to go!

I got to sit beside Bill and he offered to share his meal. Then and there I thought, *What a good guy this is.* It was the beginning of a long and wonderful relationship. How grateful I am to my brother.

Everyone liked Bill, and I liked to hang out at his place. He didn't own a car or a driver's license, so we walked a lot and talked a lot. We both had jobs. I earned fifty dollars a week as a teller at the Royal Bank in Brantford, Ontario, and Bill was making eighty-five cents an hour at Bertram's Foundry in Dundas. Work was the main focus, but our social life was filled with family gatherings and hanging out with his friends. Between home, school, and church, my social circle was small, and I didn't have close friends. I attended a small country church, Jerseyville Baptist, and Bill was happy to attend with me.

We were busy all through our engagement year—attending the weddings of many of his friends, spreading our wings, tasting freedom and the fruits of our labour. 1967 was Canada's Centennial, and Bill collected and saved one-dollar centennial bills, which he used to purchase an engagement ring for me at Birks Jewelers in Hamilton. He took me along so I could choose the ring I liked. I recall the sales clerk joking, "That's a pile of cash. Did you rob a bank?" I had to admit, it was a pile of money.

Our wedding was on May 17, 1968, and we rented an apartment in the city for ninety-eight dollars a month. We enjoyed our new home. Then came the children—two daughters, Julie and Tina—and we bought a house on Charing Cross Street in Brantford. Looking back, it is preposterous to think of the dollar values of houses compared to today. We had struggled with the decision to make an offer on the house. It would cost us $15,000, and we didn't know if we could afford that, but we agreed to make it work. And we did make it work. We signed the mortgage papers and never looked back. Those were delightful days.

After a few years, we both had a desire to roam and thought about moving west, or maybe even to Australia. I could not fathom the thought of leaving Canadian soil. Although we didn't know where, or when, or how, we made the decision to move somewhere inside our borders. Neither of us had travelled far from home, and we knew very little about the rest of the country. We believed that because it was Canada, it would be good. And it was good.

In 1977 we headed northwest—through northern Ontario, land of the silver birch and lakes and home of the beaver—and crossed into the Manitoba Prairies. Seeing the never-ending stretches of land and horizon was completely exhilarating.

"Number 1 Highway, West. We're going the right direction," I commented, as co-pilot.

This was living lightly with a dream in our heads, the proceeds from the sale of our home in our pockets, and our children in the back seat of

Loss of a Spouse

our '71 Maverick. We were riding on a cloud of hopeful expectation.

"I wonder what that sign means?" Bill asked, as we drove past a highway sign that said ORBIT AHEAD. Within the next kilometer, we saw a bin in the shape of a planet and a sign directing drivers to Put your trash into ORBIT. "Okay, so the people on the prairies have a sense of humour," we chuckled. That was a good sign.

With no particular destination in mind, we anticipated viewing the Rockies for the first time, with thoughts of pressing on into British Columbia, having heard of its beauty and grandeur. We arrived safely in Calgary, where we would seek information about employment and housing. This huge metropolis opened up for us as we wandered our way through traffic, concrete streets, and high-rise buildings.

"I wonder if we can find the employment office downtown?" Bill asked, in a way that was not especially hopeful.

"Where are the trees? There are so many one-way streets. How do we figure this out?" I asked, puzzling over the map of the city. Traffic was heavy. It was rush hour. The sense of open space and wide horizons was behind us.

Local newspapers reflected the current attitude expressed by then-mayor, Ralph Klein, who said the city was experiencing 'an influx of bums from the east'. Not the greatest welcome mat. We quickly decided to press on toward the mountains.

The Post Hotel was our resting place at Lake Louise. We marveled at the sights and sounds of springtime in the Rockies.

"This is amazing. It is so beautiful. Do you think you could find employment here?" I asked Bill.

"Well, it's a provincial park and there would be *some* work, but you can't eat the scenery," he replied.

Considering our next step, we looked at the map of Alberta and decided to drive north on Highway 93 and across the David Thompson Highway to Red Deer. We would check it out and decide from there, giving ourselves three or four days to get a feel for the surroundings. Stopping in Rocky Mountain House, I wondered if there was a Baptist church in town, while Bill wanted to know if there was a beer store. As I recall, there was a beer store but no Baptist church. Obviously, these were the two top criteria for possible relocation.

We drove on into Red Deer, checked it out, stayed the four days, and never left. It became our new home, along with a new church family, a new job for Bill, and a new neighbourhood for the children. A man we met at the church introduced Bill to the management of the Chrysler Parts Distribution Centre. He was hired and worked there for the next twenty years in the parts department. How blessed we were.

We filled the years in Westpark with our busy schedules. The girls went through school and I attended Red Deer College—working toward a degree in education. In their teen years, Julie worked at the Ponderosa restaurant and Tina was into sports of every kind, excelling in them all, especially ladies' softball. It was a full-activity calendar for all of us.

In the early nineties, Bill was slowing down. For some unknown reason, his energy level dropped significantly. For two years there seemed to be no rhyme or reason to it, with no specific diagnosis. Finally, he saw a specialist who did a number of tests and biopsies, and the outcome spelled neurofibrosarcoma, a cancer of the soft tissues.

Major surgery followed. They removed a large tumour from his abdomen, a difficult surgery to be sure. Afterwards, he was at death's door. His kidneys were failing. His skin colour was grey. His eyes were dark and his face gaunt. How I prayed every day. Visiting him in hospital became routine. The doctors told me there was nothing more they could do. I called for his family to come. He was not expected to live for much longer.

I started planning for a funeral service so that all would be in place when his family arrived. I even went to buy a 'funeral dress' to wear that day. It was overwhelming. I prayed that God would help me be strong for myself, Bill, Julie, Tina, and everyone else. God is so faithful. He provides what we need when we need it. While reading my daily devotionals, I was impressed that they were pointing to scriptures about healing and restoration. *Could God be speaking to me through these pages?* I wondered. "Dare I believe that You are giving me this word to apply in our current situation?" I asked God.

I shared what I was sensing with family members. They did not dispute the fact that the words were powerful and encouraged me to act on whatever I sensed I should do, so I called two brothers from our church, Keith and Dave Rideout, and asked them to come to the hospital to anoint Bill and pray for healing. They came and anointed him, and we left it all in the Lord's hands.

It was the start of the weekend when we offered that prayer. All was quiet and routine at the hospital. On Monday morning, the doctor came into the room and said, "What's this.... Magic?" Bill's kidneys were not shutting down; in fact, they were picking up in function, and his stats were improving. I explained that instead of magic, it could be a miracle, and told him about the anointing and prayer the previous Friday night. Remarkably, Bill continued to steadily gain strength, and on Easter Sunday, he was allowed a day pass from the hospital to attend church. I'll never forget seeing the letters on the wall of the church sanctuary declaring, "I am the resurrection and the life". These are Jesus's words—so true then, so true today, so true for eternity. We were learning to live lightly and to allow God to guide, direct, and empower us day by day. A deep sense of gratitude, hope, and joy lifted our spirits, and we celebrated that Easter like none other.

Bill went back to work. Family members returned home. We all went back to our studies and occupations. During the next five years, Bill and I enjoyed motorcycle adventures with the Central Alberta Christian Motorcyclist Association and other simple pursuits such as spending time with the family and attending lots of ballgames. Tina pitched for her softball team, and we cheered them on to many victories in provincial and national tournaments. It was a precious time.

Five years later, Bill began to sense physical discomfort. He had been taking no medication, no treatments of any kind, and seemed to be doing well. However, on a regular checkup, the doctors found returning cancer growth. This time he chose to go with chemotherapy. It was devastating to see the decline in his strength and endurance from the meds. His hair was falling out and he asked me to shave it all off. I cried while doing that, thinking about the implications that lay ahead.

We didn't know that in six months he would be gone. He never gave up hope. He thought that if he could overcome cancer once, he could do it again. The rest of us were not so sure, but we chose to support his outlook and live lightly once again, trusting God for his determination of our days. It was in the last week of his life that he accepted the fact that he was really sick. We had little time to prepare for the inevitable reality of parting. It is always a shock when the time comes, even as it was a relief for him to be released from the suffering.

The funeral was held here in Red Deer, and we also arranged for an outdoor memorial service at the Grove Cemetery in Dundas, Ontario, where we scattered some of Bill's ashes at his parents' gravesite. So many friends and relatives came to honour his life and his passing. To this day, I still have the remainder of his ashes in a box covered in the leather of his motorcycle jacket, so creatively designed by a motorcycle-riding friend. When the time comes, my ashes will be placed with his for burial. Meanwhile, I seek to live lightly. I don't want to hold on to much materially, nor be weighed down by much emotionally. I'm casting all my cares on Jesus. He is the One who allows me to live lightly.

REFLECTION

> "Yea, though I walk through the valley of the shadow of death, I will fear no evil; for Thou art with me; Your rod and staff, they comfort me."
> –Psalm 23:4

I believe the faith factor is a very important aspect of life. Thank God I had a mustard seed of faith in my subsequent journey, because the possibilities of fantasy and folly were also present.

How do dreams form in one's mind, and how are they sustained? I believe there is a God who made me, who loves me, who died for me, and who calls me to follow Him. I also believe that He gives me insight and wisdom, and new longings in my heart to know Him, His presence, and His power for each day. I want to do what I know to be pleasing to Him. The key is to ask for His ways to be made clear and then choose to do that.

After Bill's passing, I was introduced to the Seventh-day Adventist health message and started studying health and lifestyles. It makes me wonder if I had known then what I know now, how things may have been different for my husband. However, I cannot change what is past. We live in the present, ever learning and ever growing in knowledge, wisdom, and faith so that we can influence others to live in the light God has given.

APPLICATION

A. Acknowledge that life is a journey of learning.
B. Believe that God loves you, guides you, and teaches you by His Holy Spirit.
C. Claim His words as He reveals Himself to you in your everyday walk with Him.

PRAYER

Father in heaven, how grateful I am for Your presence. You are merciful. You are compassionate. You are forgiving. I know that our days are numbered on this earth. I give thanks for the experiences You have seen me through. I acknowledge my weaknesses, my need for You, my dependence on You for the air I breathe and for each breath I take.

My times are in Your hands. I pray for those who are experiencing the loss of loved ones. May Your Spirit comfort and sustain them and fill them afresh with the hope we have in Jesus Christ. Teach us how to live lightly. Amen.

Walking in the Dark

— 2 —

Light vs Darkness

I VISITED MY SISTER in New Zealand at the turn of the century, when Y2K was all the stir. The end of 1999 was approaching, and we were all anticipating the entrance of the new millennium. In the southern hemisphere in the summertime, the stars usually shine brightly, and the heavens glow with twinkling iridescence. I stayed with my sister for a month on her huge property on the North Island, an hour's drive from the town of Taihape. A veterinarian, she raised sheep and deer and kept horses, along with several dogs to help with roundups.

The landscape in this part of New Zealand, as in much of the country, consists of continuous rolling hills dotted with white polka dots of countless sheep. Living in the country, raising animals, and working to keep everything in order was an enormous challenge. This was her calling and she gave it her all. She had become familiar with all of it—the hills, the valleys, the streams, the fence lines, and the forested areas. On the high tops stood a huge communication tower. All this you could see in the daylight, and there were so many amazing vistas for me to take in and enjoy.

She sent me off with some neighbours one day to attend church. I was looking forward to sharing in the cultural distinctives of worship with the family of God in another part of the world. I spent a wonderful day together with new friends, food, and fellowship. As the sun set, darkness closed in quickly. Returning home and arriving at the gate leading to the distant farmhouse, I thanked my new acquaintances for the pleasant day and we parted. As their vehicle drove away and the lights of the car diminished, I realised I was standing in total darkness. I was at the gate, but I could not see the path.

    I had no flashlight to light my way. The sky was overcast, so no stars were shining, and there was no moonlight reflecting light from the sun. I strained to see beyond the gate. I knew the path led upward and curved toward the farmhouse, but I could not see the path. I was unsure of my next step. Step by careful step, I moved forward, painfully slowly, feeling with extended foot for a safe planting. How timid, how reluctant, how unsure was I moving in the dark. When I finally could see a glimmer of light through the branches and could focus on the distant beam, I was able to breathe easier, relax my tense muscles from head to toe, and move toward the light that was now lighting my path. This was twenty years ago, but I still remember that experience of being in the dark. What would have taken five minutes in daylight took long, painstaking moments of thought, courage, and trust. How greatly we depend on light.

REFLECTION

Light has its origin in the Word of God. The first words on record uttered by God, to our knowledge, are in Genesis 1.

> "And God said, 'Let there be light.' And there was light. And God saw the light, that it was good; and God divided the light from the darkness. God called the light Day and the darkness He called Night. So the evening and the morning were the first day."
> —Genesis 1: 3–5

> "Every good gift and every perfect gift is from above, and comes down from the Father of lights, with whom there is no shadow of turning."
> —James 1: 17

Am I grateful for the light? Do I take it for granted? Do I think about the blessing of daylight, sunlight, starlight, moonlight? Each has its own beauty and purpose. How can I express my gratitude for light?

APPLICATION

A. Acknowledge that God is the Creator of light.

Walking in the Dark

B. Believe that He created the earth and all that is in it.

C. Claim His promise as the Father of Lights, who created us for a relationship with Him. God is *love,* and the light is an expression of His love for us.

PRAYER

Our Father, which art in heaven, hallowed be Thy Name. We believe we are created by Your hand. We recognise that the earth and all that is in it comes from Your creative power. Thank you for the light. Thank you for the day and the night. Thank you for dividing the darkness from the light. Teach us how to walk in the light, to live in the light, to enjoy the light You have provided. Amen.

Riding in the Rain

– 3 –

Daytime vs Nightime

DURING THE FIVE YEARS between bouts with cancer and his death, my husband and I talked about the things we might be able to do before that day would eventually arrive. After recovering from major surgery and the removal of tumours, he took on the challenge of learning to ride a motorcycle, and I agreed to do the same. When we joined the Christian Motorcycle Association in Central Alberta, we began to 'Ride for the Son'.

Learning to Live Lightly

We travelled many miles on winding highways, enjoying the wind whistling by and the crisp and clear sounds and scents of the countryside. Learning to live lightly, we would set a destination, gather only the bare essentials for travel, and hit the road. A sense of freedom from daily concerns and worries of the world would disappear at the first rev of the engine. We shifted into gear and we were off!

The roads of Alberta tend to be very straight and uneventful, but the countryside is beautiful, and fields displaying a bountiful harvest are a sight to behold. Riding with the wind, we clocked many miles on the speedometer, and we could always count on the ride to lift our spirits and cast off cares. That was the case most of the time, but there were times of riding in the dark too.

On one such occasion, our group was invited to visit and speak at a campground an hour and a half from home. We rode to the site in daylight, but darkness settled in on our return. We had provisions for night riding of course—headlights and tail lights, and rain gear when necessary. They were all necessary that night. It would be a long, cold, and wet ride home. No wipers cleared the rain from our motorcycle windshield, nor from our helmet face guards, nor from the surface of our eyeglasses. Streams of water across all three did not make for an easy ride. Our only focus was on the tail lights of the motorcycle immediately ahead. Darkness enveloped the whole scene. Visibility was reduced to a single beam of light and the red reflection of the tail lights just ahead, while travelling at an uncommonly dangerous speed.

The Ride Captain takes on the huge responsibility of the safety of all those who follow. Light is never taken for granted. A different kind of light was needed that night—trust in our Ride Captain that he knew where he was going and that the road was safe to travel.

By God's grace, we returned home safely, but we'd learned a very important lesson. Decisions were made then and there about more thought and consideration in planning future commitments. Riding in the dark is not the same as riding in the light. The same is true for life. Living in the dark is not the same as living in the light.

REFLECTION

"Jesus said to His disciples, 'A little while longer the light is with you. Walk while you have the light, lest darkness overtake you. He who walks in darkness does not know where he is going. While you have the light, believe in the light, that you may become sons of light'."
–John 12:35

APPLICATION

A. Acknowledge your need to see clearly.

B. Believe that God is there to guide you, even in the dark

C. Claim His promise: "I will never leave you nor forsake you" (Hebrews 13:5).

PRAYER

Abba, Father, there are many things we do not see or understand. We are limited by our surroundings, our lack of knowledge, and distractions that keep us from knowing You.

Help us to seek the light. Help us to find the light hidden in Your Word. Help us to become sons and daughters of light. We want to live lightly. Amen.

Hiding in the Dark

— 4 —

Peace vs Unrest

HELPING OTHERS takes on many forms. When you consider the needs of humanity, the opportunities to give, serve, and assist are endless and enormous. So many people deserve and demand our compassionate attention and action: children dying of hunger in Africa, Soviet Jews hoping for repatriation to Israel, orphans needing nurture in India, refugees needing a safe home in Europe, citizens desiring trustworthy politicians in South America, and the poor in our own country. Thanks to a short-term mission trip, I understood more about the plight of those suffering in this world, but I wanted my understanding to lead to action. And as a widow living alone, I wanted to reshape, rebuild, and perhaps reframe my life around helping where I could.

In 2000, I travelled to Sierra Leone to observe the workings of a Christian humanitarian organization for a month. 2000 was a time of political unrest in the country, and I was very aware of the heightened level of concern for personal security and safety where I was staying. The living quarters for staff were simple, though luxurious compared to homes in the village. Every property of value was surrounded by high walls, and barbed wire curled along the tops of concrete barriers to discourage entry. It was common to have a night watchman on duty. The hired help was provided a small room in which to live, and the "kitchen" was an outdoor firepit.

Grocery shopping was a far cry from what I experience in Canadian supermarkets. We took turns walking the few miles to the nearest shop to purchase the food we needed. I remember resting for a few moments on a large rock along the road to relieve my cramped muscles from gripping the bags of groceries. I vowed to never again complain about going for groceries in Canada, where I could drive to and from a grocery store quickly and easily at any time and fill the car with as much as I wanted.

Any white person in the village was a novelty, and often the children would run alongside us, pointing and sometimes calling out words that I didn't understand. It was better not to know what they were saying. I would smile in response.

In the village, loud speakers blasted out messages vying for people's attention and allegiance. The unrest and uncertainty could be felt everywhere. On occasion, the staff would travel to the inner city, where the evidence of power-seeking corruption and hostility appeared most obvious. Bullet holes were visible in government buildings and business offices. Currency exchanges were arranged through a friend of a friend at a pre-arranged time, with pre-identified persons, in an alley.

Clothing, tools, and much-needed equipment had been collected and sent to the organization by sea container from Canada, and unloading and moving the contents from the shipping container to our location was a great challenge. Things went missing and would appear in the marketplace for sale. The frustration of the work was ever present.

The most disturbing times were when loud voices shouting, "Rebels! Rebels!" could be heard in the distance. It was a warning cry in the neighbourhood, alerting villagers to take refuge in safe places, wherever those might be. As expatriates, we were instructed to have an escape plan if necessary. *Wow!* That was less than reassuring. The plan was to run to the British Embassy to seek refuge. Finding our way in the dark was unthinkable. We huddled silently in our darkened compound and prayed for safety.

REFLECTION

When we consider man's inhumanity to man and the desire for power, profit, and control, we are driven to our knees to pray. We live in a world where sin corrupts the original plan of God. Selfishness and self-preservation take the stage. Our only hope is a change of heart, a conversion, a transformation on the spiritual level. This, in turn, is lived out in the reality of the mind and body.

Hiding in the Dark

> "Keep your heart with all diligence, for out of it spring the issues of life."
> —Proverbs 4:23
>
> "Have I not wept for him who was in trouble? Has not my soul grieved the poor? But when I looked for good, evil came to me. And when I waited for light, then came darkness. My heart is in turmoil and cannot rest."
> —Job 30: 25-27

Many struggling victims of inhumanity have sought empathy and compassion in the life story of Job. We have all tasted the fruit of the tree of the knowledge of good and evil, so we seek relief. We seek a Saviour. We need to be rescued from our fateful condition. This is precisely why Jesus came as Messiah, Deliverer, and Redeemer.

> "Before the physical malady could be healed, Christ must bring relief to the mind and cleanse the soul from sin."
> – Ellen G. White, The Ministry of Healing[1]

APPLICATION

A. Acknowledge my need and self-interest, my desire for self-preservation.

B. Believe that Jesus came to save us.

C. Claim the promises of His power to overcome evil and of His purposes to be lived out in my life, by the power of the Holy Spirit. Ask for and receive the Holy Spirit. This is learning to live lightly.

PRAYER

Our heavenly Father, we come into Your presence with heavy hearts, hearts struggling with the news and knowledge of inhumanity. We see the results of violence. We hear the cries of the people. We are disturbed by the unrest in the nations. We ask You to cleanse our hearts from sin. We ask for the presence of Your Holy Spirit. Fill us afresh this day with Your light. Amen.

Endnotes

[1] Ellen G. White, *The Ministry of Healing: Health and Happiness* (Better Living Publications, Revised ed., 1990), 24.

It's about Your Health

— 5 —

Light vs Heavy

WHAT IS YOUR WEIGHT? Do you readily share that information or do you cringe knowing the truthful answer? The Standard American Diet (SAD) has produced a population of over-weight men and women, including myself. It is clearly visible to all but excruciatingly painful to admit. Yes, I am obese according to the BMI chart. I am not happy with that label, and many times throughout my life I have given specific attention to, and made an effort to make changes. It is not easy.

Light feels better. Light looks better. Being lightweight is healthier overall. We are fearfully and wonderfully made. Our bodies are magnificent in design, in interconnectedness, in operational efficiency. They have an enormous capacity for creativity and productivity. God has designed us to 'live lightly' on a simple plan of nature's produce of vegetables, fruits, grains, and nuts. All of these are whole foods, rich in nutrients, and they come from the soil, from the roots, and from the branch.

Man tends to corrupt what God has provided. We know the manufacturing of processed food strips away nutrients, adds calories, and substitutes flavour-enhancing, addictive ingredients to compel the consumer to satisfy many cravings.

In 2017, I joined Bright Line Eating and made a commitment to follow a new plan focused on healthy eating by establishing 'bright lines'—creating a new mindset and boundaries to achieve a goal to be happy, thin, and free. I started at 222 lbs. and began the weight loss journey to an amazing 185. Yes, this felt good, looked good, was good. But I didn't want to continue. I was craving the sweets. I wanted to snack, so I did. I lost my focus. I returned to my previous eating habits. I began to regain what I had lost. No surprise. I wanted to eat the comfort foods, so I did.

There is a strong psychological aspect attached to eating, and it was overriding my desire and commitment to meet and maintain my goal. I'm into year three since the weight loss and I'm at 210 lbs., and I want to live more lightly for my health and for my happiness. I want to consider those 'bright lines' again and stake a claim for health and well-being, acknowledging that some foods are off limits—known as NMF, not my food. It's a change in mindset. It's a change in attitude. It's asking myself to be honest and truthful about what is right and good for me. Can I really live a lifestyle saying no to flour, sugar, and snacks? What if I decided to say yes to living lightly?

REFLECTION

"I beseech you therefore brethren, by the mercies of God, that you present your bodies a living sacrifice, holy, acceptable to God, which is your reasonable service. And do not be

> conformed to this world, but be transformed by the renewing of your mind, that you may prove what is that good and acceptable and perfect will of God."
> —Romans 12:1-2
>
> "Daniel purposed in his heart that he would not defile himself."
> —Daniel 1:8
>
> God said, "See, I have given you every herb that yields seed which is on the face of all the earth, and every tree whose fruit yields seed; to you it shall be for food."
> —Genesis 1:29

APPLICATION

A. Acknowledge that you are the one who must choose to make a commitment to your own health.
B. Believe in the process. Purpose in your heart. Pray.
C. Claim the success that awaits you.

PRAYER

Father God, I am willing but not able to do this on my own. I am praying for a new mindset that helps me to say yes to what is good for me and no to what is not my food. I purpose in my heart to follow the light that has been given to me. May the 'bright lines' shine ever so clearly in my decisions each day. Thank You for Your power and Your presence. Amen.

Health Education

— 6 —

Health vs Disease

I'VE BEEN ON A HEALTH and wellness journey since 2013. In the fall of that year, I enrolled in the BSc in Nursing program at Red Deer College and completed the first year. It took a lot of effort, time, and money to get there—I had already spent a couple of years at the local high school achieving the math and science requirements for entrance to the program.

After completing the first year in the nursing program, I realised that nursing was not the direction I wanted to pursue, so I withdrew. It was a difficult choice, but deep down I was relieved and had 'a peace that would endure'. I was still seeking a path to health, one that would be simple and straightforward. I was open to following the Lord and sharing the message of His love, His teaching, His Word, and His way to health and hope.

I decided to sign up to become a lifestyle coach with iHeal Canada, an organisation that teaches the eight laws of natural health using the acronym NEWSTART (nutrition, exercise, water, sunshine, temperance, air, rest, and trust in God). The method they follow is simple yet profound. Each topic is thoroughly researched and applied to daily living. I also read much about Ellen G. White and read much of what she wrote, especially her book *The Ministry of Healing*. In it she writes about the importance of being a medical missionary—taking the message of God's plan for health and healing to a hurting world. This made sense to me.

I committed to watching health documentaries to glean knowledge and understanding from others. Never before have I seen such a voluminous amount of information available for the layperson and the professional. My path led to the next level of instruction, which was to enroll in the online Durham School of Health and

Nutrition, and I was able to achieve the designation of Certified Natural Nutritionist. Other leaders in this field provide a wealth of scientific and practical application that everyone can access easily. (A list of a few of these people and resources may be found in the back of this book.)

Health and wholeness come from an effort to address the complete person—body, mind, and spirit—because the conditions of mind and spirit show up in the body. We need to have an open mind and always be willing to learn from experience, and from others, how to achieve positive outcomes. History can teach us many lessons, but we have to study it to find its nuggets of truth.

Personal discipline is a necessary ingredient in bringing about any changes required, and I've found that my online community helps me with this. We need each other to win. We need a support community to encourage us along the way. We need to believe in order to achieve. Writing this book is a big commitment for me, but I felt the need to share what I have learned with readers who also want to learn how to live lightly. Each one of us has a story to tell. Each one of us can influence others by sharing our experiences and knowledge in how to care for our world and its inhabitants.

> ### REFLECTION
>
> *"You formed my inward parts; You covered me in my mother's womb. I will praise You for I am fearfully and wonderfully made. Marvelous are your works."*
> *–Psalm 139:13, 14*
>
> *"Thy Word is a lamp unto my feet and a light unto my path."*
> *–Psalm 119:105*

In following the path of natural remedies and healthy lifestyle, I have found that much wisdom is available for those who seek it. Our current allopathic model for healthcare in North America is focused on the drug industry and deals with alleviating symptoms rather than finding the cause of disease and making the required changes. This may be an oversimplification, but it gives power to the individual to take responsibility for his or her personal health. We need light on this subject. We need voices to speak up. We need to hear from those who have been successful in regaining and maintaining health when the current models

Health Education

of health have no answers. There is hope. There is a battle to be won. May the light prevail over the darkness. Let's learn to live lightly.

APPLICATION

A. Acknowledge the fact that our health is our own responsibility.

B. Believe that you can make a change in your lifestyle that will benefit your health.

C. Claim the information and support you can access from the agencies and people who can help you.

PRAYER

Father God, we know that we are fearfully and wonderfully made. Your Word instructs us to be temperate in our ways, to care for our bodies, to refresh our minds with Your truth. Help us to seek and to find the true lamp that lights our path. Amen.

My Own Family

— 7 —

Mom vs Doctors

IN THE EARLY MONTHS of 2019, my daughter, who had suffered with Crohn's disease for several years, became increasingly ill. Following consultations with her family doctor, an internal medicine specialist, and a surgeon, it was recommended that her entire colon be removed. This procedure seemed drastic to me, but I was sure that the necessary lifestyle changes could and would make a difference if applied. We knew it would take time and a concerted effort, perhaps even a couple of years; but I believed then, and still believe now, that the natural remedies approach is the best. However, she opted for immediate surgery.

The surgery was successful. She managed elimination via an ileostomy, a bag attached to the end of the small intestine that exits the body through the abdomen. She handled all of this well, and she was very grateful for the freedom from the discomfort and pain of her Crohn's disease. Then came a further challenge. The doctors had sent the removed tissue for testing, and cancerous cell tissue was found in three spots. There was a lot of inflammation in the diseased tissue, and her colon had been degenerating over a long period. That was obvious. But the next recommendation was to begin chemotherapy as a preventative procedure against further cancer growth. I was devastated.

This was a big decision for my daughter. Should she go with the expert doctors or listen to her mother? I was all for encouraging nature's way of eating healthy and building up the immune system, but when fear of death enters the picture, the decision-making becomes intense. She chose the chemo route.

The timeframe given was several months or eight rounds of chemo. The first two rounds were tolerable. As time went by, she experienced a

My Own Family

slowdown, an increase of pain, and a growing concern for effectively managing the symptoms of stress on her body, mind, and spirit.

At a particularly low point, she called me and wondered what she should do as her pain was continuous and she was not eating or drinking anything. At this point my trust level for conventional medicine was at an all-time low, and I took her, with great concern, to emergency, where she was admitted and kept for further examination and treatment. She was dehydrated and her kidneys were functioning at 22 percent. Not a good report.

She was placed on an IV immediately to stabilise her electrolytes and kidney function. Her eyes were dark. Her skin was pale. Her energy level was at zero. Chemotherapy treatments were halted, and she was monitored closely for stabilization. A month later, the doctors decided she had gained enough strength to be discharged. Not surprisingly, the oncologist recommended continuing the chemo regimen. We asked a number of questions about making adjustments in the dosage, and he agreed to lessen the potency of the chosen formula but to continue and complete the remaining rounds. She did complete the therapy. She is now waiting for an MRI to determine whether or not there is evidence of any cancerous tissue.

REFLECTION

"When you are desponding, close the lips firmly to men; do not shadow the paths of others; but tell everything to Jesus. Reach up your hands for help. In your weakness lay hold of infinite strength. Ask for humility, wisdom, courage, increase of faith, that you may see light, in God's light and rejoice in His love."
—Ellen G. White, Ministry of Healing, 223

When we shine the light on health issues, we know that an ounce of prevention is worth a pound of cure. We know that living a healthy lifestyle promotes a healthy immune system, which takes care of all aspects of our body's inner workings. The body was created and designed to be strong and active and healthy, to do its own repair work when given the necessary ingredients. Nutrition in! Toxins out! We must learn what it takes to be good to ourselves and not be deceived or persuaded into a state of ill health by advertisements and commercial enterprises.

My Own Family

So many individuals, groups, and organizations have been shining the light on health issues recently. Documentaries and health summits abound, declaring the dangers of adopting a fast-food mentality. Depending on processed foods results in a society's drug-induced apathy toward accepting responsibility for its own health.

APPLICATION

A. Acknowledge responsibility for the state of your health. You didn't arrive here by chance.

B. Believe that the body responds well to God-given laws of a healthy lifestyle. Many conditions can be reversed and new health obtained.

C. Claim the wisdom that abounds for your benefit. "Ask, and it will be given to you; seek, and you will find; knock, and it will be opened to you" (Matthew 7:7).

PRAYER

Father, you are the Great Physician. You are our healer. You have promised to carry us, to bear our burdens. Sometimes we don't want to ask. We don't want to seek. We don't want to knock. Help us to be willing to submit and surrender to Your will so that our hearts are aligned with You and Your purposes.

Help us to see the light. Help us to come to the light. We pray in the name of Jesus, of whom it was spoken by Isaiah the prophet, "Surely He has borne our griefs and carried our sorrows; yet we esteemed Him stricken, smitten by God, and afflicted. But He was wounded for our transgressions. He was bruised for our iniquities; The chastisement for our peace was upon Him, and by His stripes we are healed" (Isaiah 53:1–5). Teach us, Father, the meaning of this statement, and help us to live in the light of Your counsel. Amen.

Boundaries

— 8 —

Saying Yes vs Saying No

FOR MORE THAN TEN YEARS, I offered rides to and from church to an elderly couple. We drove together week by week, rain or shine, spring, summer, fall, and winter. The relationship between this man and woman is unique. She is limited in vision and he is deaf. You might say they are an odd couple, in a kind way. I raised the concern about my time and the possibility of helping me with money for gas. I do recall receiving a contribution to that end a few times, for which I was grateful. I thought that receiving payment would help justify my efforts; however, I came to realise that no amount of money can make up for a resentful relationship. And that's what I was dealing with within myself.

The couple lived in an apartment building, caring for themselves as best they could. The wife had regularly scheduled appointments for kidney dialysis every Monday, Wednesday, and Friday. She was able to manage getting the help she needed for transport those days, the treatments, and other activities too. However, her health was weakening and her needs increased. Changes needed to be made, perhaps in the form of additional help, professional assessments, or some kind of intervention. The Bible says not to grow weary in well-doing, but I was coming to the end of my 'happy to help you' thinking. Why would I continue to respond to calls for help while feeling this way?

Previously, I had spent four years in a program called Celebrate Recovery, declaring at each meeting that I am a grateful Christian, struggling with codependency. What is codependency, and how does it show up in my life? It shows up when I can't say no, and I 'can't' because there is a war going on in my head between why I need to say yes and why I want to say no. For some reason, I always thought I had to be the one these people needed and depended on. This was not true. There are always others who can come alongside. I needed to confront my thoughts and I needed to explore the possibilities of sharing the task of caring and responding less often to requests for help.

When I'm asked for help these days, I ask myself, *Whose responsibility is this? Is it mine? Who else needs to be called upon?* That's a start in creating healthy boundaries for my mental health and possibly saving a relationship before it is destroyed. Enforcing healthy boundaries is a great risk for a codependent person because if the relationship ends, the yes person accepts the blame for it. This isn't realistic, but the damage is a burden.

In the famous chapter on love in the Bible, 1 Corinthians 13, I know I'm not that person exemplified in the verses. Let me explain my thinking....

It is a good thing to love your neighbour as yourself

It is a good thing to be a good Samaritan.

> It is a good thing to serve the poor and needy.
>
> It is a good thing to share your resources with others.
>
> It is a good thing to take time to listen, to encourage, to pray for others.
>
> It is a good thing to lend a helping hand

> It is not a good thing to ignore boundaries.
>
> It is not a good thing to allow others to control and manipulate.
>
> It is not a good thing to allow a victim mentality to rule.
>
> It is not a good thing to blame others for your miserable attitude.
>
> It is not a good thing to whine and complain about your status or station in life.

Why would I continue to respond to calls for help while feeling this growing resentment? Well, a number of questions come to the surface when I reflect long and hard about my thoughts, feelings, and behaviour.

What does it mean to be a Christian?

What does it mean to go the extra mile?

What does it mean when I say, "I want to be like Jesus?"

What does it mean to be challenged to love the least, the lost, and the lonely?

What does it mean to do for others what you would have them do for you?

What does it mean when you say, "It is better to give than to receive?"

What does it mean to bear one another's burdens?

What does it mean to be my brother's keeper?

Jesus said, "Greater love has no one than this, than to lay down his life for his friends."

REFLECTION

Codependency has certain traits. There is a pay-off for both sides. So I need to explore the pay-off for me in continuing this behaviour of answering the call for help when it becomes burdensome. This is where the light shines in. How open and honest can I be? Okay. I want to be seen as a loving Christian, going the extra mile. But that feeds my ego. It does not glorify Christ. I want to prove that I am willing and able to do many things. This feeds my pride. I go out of my way to volunteer. I soak up the affirmation that comes my way. I am self-righteous and gather up and store the glory for myself. My holier-than-thou attitude is revealed in my resentment. I need repentance. I need forgiveness and I need to forgive. I need to step back in humility and surrender my life, my attitude, and my journey to the Lord. I don't like what I see. I don't like where I am.

What happens when the caregiver needs care?

What needs to be confronted when the relationship is strained?

Turn to Scripture.

> *The elders who are among you I exhort. I who am a fellow elder and a witness of the sufferings of Christ, and also a partaker of the glory that will be revealed: Shepherd the flock of God which is among you, serving as overseers, not by compulsion but willingly, not for dishonest gain, but eagerly; nor as being lords over those entrusted to you, but being examples to the flock; and when the Chief Shepherd*

appears, you will receive the crown of glory that does not fade away.

Likewise, you younger people, submit yourselves to your elders. Yes, all of you be submissive to one another, and be clothed with humility. For God resists the proud, but gives grace to the humble. Therefore humble yourselves under the mighty hand of God, that He may exalt you in due time, casting all your cares upon Him for He cares for you. Be sober and vigilant because your adversary the devil walks about like a roaring lion seeking whom he may devour. Resist him, steadfast in the faith, knowing that the same sufferings are experienced by your brotherhood in the world.

But may the God of all grace, who called us to His eternal glory by Christ Jesus, after you have suffered a while, perfect, establish, strengthen, and settle you. To Him be the glory and the dominion forever and ever. Amen.
−1 Peter 5:1–11

APPLICATION

A. Acknowledge my need for repentance. I repent.

B. Believe God forgives me and loves me. He gives me the power to forgive and the power to love.

C. Claim His forgiveness and rest in His promises. He restores. He recovers. He reshapes. He rebuilds. He is in the refining business. He is refining me.

PRAYER

Father, thank you for your Holy Spirit. "Greater is He that is in me than he that is in the world" (1 John 4:4).

Your mercy is great and your compassion is extended to all. As far as the east is from the west, so far have you removed our transgressions from us (Psalm 103:12) We come as Your children, repenting of our selfish ways. How grateful we are that You receive us and do not cast us away. We behold Jesus on the cross—extending forgiveness to His murderers and crying out to You, "Father, forgive them for they know not what they do."

We must take a stand in this generation for the truth, for what is right, for what is good. Help us, Lord, to resist the evil one. In our own strength we can do nothing, but by Your Spirit, all things are possible. We submit and surrender this day to Your will and Your ways. Teach us, Lord. Lead us, Lord. Empower us to rise above the darkness and to walk in the light. Help us in our learning to live lightly. Amen.

Stepping Up, Speaking Up

— 9 —

Boldness vs Timidity

I ARRIVED EARLY at the Anchorage airport, well ahead of the time for check-in. My flight was scheduled for 2:30 a.m., and there was another flight to Seattle prior to mine leaving from the same gate. I was prepared to sit and relax, maybe read a bit before boarding. As passengers gathered for the earlier flight, I became aware of a family nearby, eagerly waiting to board the plane. Three generations were together—an elderly couple, the son or daughter and spouse, and a young grandchild. I later learned the man was eighty-eight years old and his wife eighty-six. This elderly gentleman was seated in a wheelchair, and he carried an oxygen machine on his lap, with the nasal cannula connecting the machine to his nostrils. It was obvious he would be considered a person needing some assistance.

Just prior to their boarding time, an airline agent approached the gentleman and began to explain that she was very sorry but there was a problem with him boarding the plane with his oxygen machine. Apparently, the machine he was using was not a model that was listed in their policy book as one that was approved by the airline. The whole family was shocked to hear this message, and much discussion ensued amongst themselves.

"How could this be? "questioned the elderly man. He had travelled previously with the same machine and it hadn't been a problem. "Why now?"

The agent explained that she couldn't give an answer as to why he had been allowed to travel with this machine on other flights but that it was their policy and they had to follow the rules.

As the implications of the matter began to sink in, the tension rose and the conversation grew louder and more emotional. Anger, frustration, confusion, and fear took centre stage. The adult children did their best to calm the parents, to no avail. The elderly man asked to speak with the airline agent's supervisor, and so another customer service rep came along to further clarify the policy and support his colleague. A long explanation and discussion followed about how this couple would be expected to meet the requirements to board the flight to Seattle.

They were offered a shuttle service to a local hotel that evening and a voucher to cover their stay. The following day, they needed to buy an oxygen machine which would be one from the list approved by the airline, find a doctor, and have the doctor write a letter stating that the oxygen machine he would be travelling with was approved. The airline would also provide coupons for their taxi fare back to the airport.

At this point, I was thinking that these airline reps believed this to be a very generous offer to the couple, but I began to imagine the degree of stress this man and woman were experiencing because of these demands. Frustration was rising. Where could they find a doctor? How would they get a different machine? I heard them discuss the implications.

"This machine cost us $1,700 and we can't afford to buy another one."

"How can we find a doctor?"

"How can we find a machine?"

"How can we get around?"

"How can we get home if our family leaves us here?"

There didn't seem to be any answers. The boarding time for their scheduled flight was announced. Nothing had been settled. The younger family realised they had to make a decision for themselves and decided to board the plane. They told their parents,

"Just do what you have to do. You have to follow the rules. It will be okay."

With that said, they *left them!* I couldn't believe it. More discussion followed with the airline service reps.

They repeated, "This is the policy. These are the rules. This is what you must do."

They repeated the steps they expected them to take to comply. The elderly man insisted that he had travelled previously with no problem.

"Why is it a problem now, and why had no one made us aware of this machine being unacceptable?" he demanded.

The agent still could not answer his question but stuck to the policy. Blood pressures were rising, both his, his wife's, and mine. Sitting in silence, listening to the whole conversation, and following the scenario from the start, I began to pray, asking God for wisdom. My thoughts raced. *This should not be happening. Should I intervene? What would I say? Is it my business? What in the world did I think that I could do?* Still arguing with myself, I stood up and approached the two airline reps and explained that I had overheard the discussion and realised that there was a crisis evolving and escalating, and I wondered if I could get some clarification and perhaps assist in some way.

We spoke about the risks involved.

"Was it a risk to the airline or a risk for other travellers to allow this man with his oxygen machine on the plane?" was my first question.

It seemed like the risk to the airline was minimal. The agent was concerned that should something happen to the man while in flight, he, the agent, would be held responsible for not following policy. Yes, I could understand that.

"However, "I explained, "if you are really concerned about this man's welfare, I think the stress that is being placed on him at the moment is causing far greater likelihood of possible stroke or heart attack than his oxygen machine that is working just fine. Perhaps you need to look at changing the policy or at making an exception in this situation."

I decided to add a challenging element to the conversation, so I mentioned that I was sure the CEO of the airline would not want any adverse publicity concerning customer care and service.

We focused on the problem again. What was it about the model of the machine that was unacceptable? It seemed that an upgraded version was in the policy manual and as far as I understood, it had to do with oxygen production and capacity. His machine was a number 4 and the new requirement was a number 5.

I don't know if it referred to liters of oxygen prescribed or something else, but I suggested that the difference between 4 liters of oxygen and 5 liters of oxygen would not be reason enough to decline boarding an aircraft. I also suggested he call his superiors or local physicians to get their input since this was an unnecessary burden for the couple to deal with.

I left him thinking about that and said I would go and speak to the couple and try to calm and comfort them, which I did. I approached them and assured them that I had overheard the discussions and understood their difficulty. I agreed that the whole situation seemed outrageous and something needed to be done for them.

I asked if it would be alright to pray with them. They agreed, thanking me. So, on my knees in front of these two, I prayed the most earnest prayer I could muster, thanking God for these dear people and for God's provision for our lives and for His faithfulness in all things. I asked God to intervene on their behalf and thanked Him for hearing our prayer.

I offered a few more words of encouragement and went back to my seat, not knowing what would happen. The airline rep was on his cell phone. He talked a long time, looking away, looking back, then talking again. Finally, he approached me and said that he had contacted five different doctors and inquired about their recommendations on the different oxygen machine models. He was 95 percent certain that the slight difference between the 4 and the 5 model would not be a great concern and need not keep the couple from boarding the plane.

I thanked him for taking the time and trouble to get that recommendation and said that it was the right thing to do. Inside, my heart was dancing the hallelujah chorus. God is good. He moves in marvellous ways, His wonders to perform. And He used me to speak up and then He performed a miracle.

The rep shared the news with the couple, the wife now in tears and the husband with his head lowered to his chest in exhaustion and unspeakable relief. The rep spoke to me again and thanked me for speaking up on behalf of this aged couple. He promised to take personal responsibility in making policy changes whenever such a need would arise.

I think he was somewhat concerned about the possibility of bad publicity and wanted to make sure I was satisfied with the outcome also. So be it. This precious couple was on the next flight and headed home. So was I. God is good! This was the highlight of my trip. I was living lightly.

REFLECTION

There are times when we must step up, speak up, and bring matters to the light. We may not have answers, but questions help to clarify. A calm and peaceful attitude sets the tone.

> *"Where there is no counsel, the people fall; but in the multitude of counselors there is safety."*
> *—Proverbs 11:14*

It is wise to seek greater understanding and bring greater authority to bear concerning an issue. It is wise to seek solutions. It is possible to bring hope and encouragement by coming alongside. It is never wrong to ask the Holy Spirit to intervene with wisdom.

APPLICATION

A. Acknowledge the reality, the issue, the difficulties.

B. Believe there is a peaceful path to seek resolution.

C. Claim the promise of God to give wisdom. Seek Him. Seek His ways and His truth in the matter. This is learning to live lightly.

PRAYER

Father God, Your wisdom is unsearchable. You make a way when there is no way. You hear the cry of Your children. You answer. We thank you and praise You for Your goodness. I pray for this experience to be a lasting one for this elderly couple. May they always remember that our lives are in Your hands. You will see us home. Help us always to live in the light of this hope. Amen.

Darby and the Soup Kitchen

— 10 —

Love vs Indifference

SEEKING THE LOST is what God does. Someone I know does the same. His name is Darby, and he's a volunteer at the Red Deer soup kitchen. He has a heart for people who are hurting and makes a huge effort to contact those who, out of necessity, find themselves on the streets of our city.

Each Thursday and Saturday, a hot meal is provided at suppertime, and on the first two Sundays of each month, breakfast is served. He does his 'walkabout' on those days, handing out cards reminding people of the times and the place to come for a meal. He makes a certain loop to check on possible spots where he might find his friends. Often there is an opportunity to chat. He'll offer a coffee at McDonalds and find out how things are going.

During the COVID-19 crisis, our dining hall was reorganised as a takeout centre. We installed a half-door barricade at the front with space to pass out a lunch bag. As a safeguard, we put Plexiglass above that space and marked spaces for social distancing inside and outside. We wanted to protect the volunteers and those in need of the free meal.

The needs are real. People still get hungry. We still have an obligation and a desire to meet these real needs. My question is how does one learn to live lightly on the streets? Anxiety and safety are constant issues for this population. Of all people, these individuals know that life is reduced to staying in survival mode and finding a place to sleep, something to wear, and food to eat. Not an easy life. Is there light at the end of this tunnel? What light can we offer?

There are social networks for assistance. We can point to these. We can offer words of encouragement and greet each person cheerfully. We can brighten the day with a smile. We can pray. Darby does all of these.

He told me once of his interaction with a young person, a newcomer to the city, and how even a brief encounter can make a difference for eternity. Darby met him, before COVID-19 shut things down, in the downtown library in February 2020 while Darby was making his usual rounds. The young man was sitting at a table holding a loaf of bread. Darby spoke with him, asked a few questions, and offered to buy him a hot drink. (Darby calls this his 'hot drink ministry'.) The young man welcomed the kind gesture and they began to chat. He gave Darby a fictitious name, something from a character in a video game. No problem. Many people would rather remain anonymous. (For the rest of the story I will refer to this new friend as 'Gamer'.) Darby gave him one of his cards with the address of the soup kitchen and the times that meals would be served.

Later that day, Gamer arrived at the door an hour early, talking so quickly it seemed that he was in an altered state of mind—perhaps on meds, perhaps on drugs. Sometimes there are medical issues, sometimes mental issues, sometimes both. He needed a change of clothes, hygiene products, socks, and underwear. Being on the street means there is no access to showers or laundry facilities. Life gets hard quickly. Darby outfitted Gamer with the best that was on hand. There is not a big supply kept on site, but donations come in from time to time. Handouts are given as needed.

Gamer shared a bit of his story with Darby. He had been living in British Columbia as a foster kid. The plan was to find and meet his biological parents, who were apparently in Red Deer. He had also broken up with a girlfriend recently, and it seemed a good idea to find new opportunities. Coming to Red Deer was the plan. He expected his parents to come to the soup kitchen to meet him. They didn't show.

Darby has a heart for kids who are struggling in life. He knows how hard it can be. He talks of writing a book one day, when the time is right. His empathy is felt. People trust him fairly quickly. He asked Gamer if he could put his name on his prayer list. Gamer agreed and thanked him for his thoughts and concern.

Darby has a supply of easy-to-read books by George R. Knight, one of them entitled *God's Truth*.[2] They read through the first chapter together, and then Gamer left to find a place for the night. Two weeks later, Darby saw Gamer and asked how things were going. It was good. He had a place to stay and was receiving some social assistance.

The next time Gamer appeared in the lineup at the door for supper, it was the 7th of May. He was clean and nicely dressed, but he shared with Darby that he was back at the shelter on the mat program, where they provide sleeping space for those on the street. He said he was participating in a twelve-step recovery program and wondered if Darby would consider being his sponsor. Gamer gave Darby his real name and opened up in an honest discussion about dealing with depression. He wanted to get on the right path. He wanted to do better. He needed help and was asking for it.

It was the last time Darby would ever talk with his new friend. Gamer died four hours later. His death was believed to be an accidental overdose or a bad combination of street drugs. No one knows for sure. Bad news travels fast, and Darby heard the rumors and checked the obituary column online. It was his friend. It was true. It was a sad loss.

REFLECTION

I asked Darby, "How do you learn to live lightly in the midst of these challenging realities?"

He said, "We keep doing what we're doing. It's important to be here." He went on to offer some feedback, words he'd received from the street population. "They (the people on the street) say we are different (referring to our soup kitchen volunteers). They say we care. They say the food is good. We offer things they need. They say the hardest part is not connecting with mainstream society. Often they feel ignored, looked down on, and unworthy of acceptance." Mental health issues, family issues, and homelessness compound and create barriers so difficult to overcome.

Darby's vision is to provide not only a handout but a hand up. He has a vision for building an apartment complex to provide affordable housing, healthy food, and medical care—a safe place to live. He dreams of a community of faith where all are accepted and are able to worship freely in a non-judgemental environment where everyone is welcome and all can participate. That is how he is living in the light of hope. He's praying for others to come alongside him until the dream becomes a reality.

You could be part of that dream coming true. Our website is reddeersoupkitchen.ca. Donations can be made online through Canadahelps.org or sent to our mailing address: Red Deer Soup Kitchen, P.O. Box 431, Red Deer, AB T4N 5E9.

Bless you for your heart to help.

> *Though I bestow all my goods to feed the poor, and though I give my body to be burned, but have not love it profits me nothing. Love suffers long and is kind; love does not envy; love does not parade itself, is not puffed up; does not behave rudely, does not seek its own, is not provoked, thinks no evil; does not rejoice in iniquity, but rejoices in truth; bears all things, believes all things, hopes all things, endures all things. Love never fails.*
>
> *But whether there are prophecies, they will fail; whether there are tongues, they will cease; whether there is knowledge, it will vanish away. For we know in part and*

we prophesy in part. But when that which is perfect has come, then that which is in part will be done away. When I was a child, I spoke as a child, I understood as a child, I thought as a child; but when I became a man, I put away childish things.

For now we see in a mirror dimly, but then face to face. Now I know in part, but then I shall know just as I also am known. And now abide faith, hope, and love, these three; but the greatest of these is love.
–1 Corinthians 13: 1–13

APPLICATION

A. Acknowledge the real needs around you. Look past the fault to see the need.

B. Believe that God values everyone, no matter what, and He calls us to be His sons and daughters of light in a dark world.

C. Claim His truth for yourself, and share that same truth so others may come to the light. The Light of the World is *Jesus*.

PRAYER

Abba, Father, we grieve the loss of one of Your children. We know the challenges are great. We can't always make things happen the way we think they should. We pray for Your Holy Spirit to move us to actions that would be helpful. We pray for protection for those who are seeking to do the best they can with what they have. Help us all, Lord, to be aware, to empathise, to listen, to learn, to obey Your voice as You direct our steps. Help us all to learn to live in such a manner that we reflect the light of Your love, no matter what. Amen.

Endnotes

[2] George R. Knight, *God's Truth: Can Change Your Life* (Columbia, MD: Pacific Press Publishing Association, 2020).

A Place in the Country

— 11 —

City vs Country Living

FROM THE HIGH RIDGES of the landscape of Central Alberta, you can look west to the mountains and east to the prairies. It is known as Big Sky Country. We were on a search again. It was time to make another move. My daughter Julie and I were searching for an acreage somewhere outside the city.

During the previous three months, I had my half-duplex listed for sale. I had planned to downsize, move to a condo in the city, and enjoy my retirement days. I found a place that was lovely, just right for me. I made an offer subject to selling my home. It didn't happen. COVID-19 entered the picture. Everything shut down. No calls. No inquiries. No open house opportunities to show my home. No sale. No condo.

It was during the third month after listing that the message and meaning of country living began to grow in my thoughts, and my concerns for the future took on greater focus. I started thinking about moving to the country with Julie, a single-mom daughter, and her three teenage boys instead of living by myself and paying condo fees. My thinking was that perhaps together, we could purchase a home big enough to accommodate us all and provide ourselves a new lifestyle that would prompt a whole new era of sustainability. Julie would be retiring from her city job in the next five years. The boys were at the age where they needed to gain skills and think about how to make a living. I had my own dreams of how I might best use my knowledge and experience in health and nutrition to further my dream of having a business called Health and Hope Ministries.

A Place in the Country

Because of the COVID-19 pandemic, we were in the midst of a global lockdown. Wearing masks and social distancing had become the norm for many. As a Seventh-day Adventist, I knew of Ellen. G. White's warnings and admonitions for God's people to move to the country, away from the cities. One of her books in her Spirit of Prophecy series[3] points to a time when the world will be shaken, a time when we may be restricted from buying and selling, and we would need to be prepared. I was listening. I was wondering. I was seeking God's guidance. He brought a few things to mind.

William Carey, a Baptist missionary to India in 1793, said, "Expect great things from God. Attempt great things for God." A life submitted and surrendered to the Lord is a life of walking in His light. He knows. He guides. He provides. We need to commit and cooperate. Yes, God has given me a brain to use, and I submit that too, along with my will. Scripture says, "My sheep hear my voice and I know them, and they follow Me" (John 10:27). I am listening and letting His light shine on my path.

The parable in the Bible that tells of a merchant seeking beautiful pearls says he found one pearl of great price, went and sold all that he had, and bought it (Matthew 13:45–46). Another parable is similar: "The Kingdom of heaven is like treasure hidden in a field, which a man found and hid; and for joy over it he goes and sells all that he has and buys that field" (Matthew 13:44).

I am confidently watching and waiting for the Lord to help us find our way in this matter. The outcome is His. The future is unknown, but His promises are sure. We can live lightly in expectation of His leading, understanding that the real treasure is Jesus Himself.

REFLECTION

"Being confident of this very thing, that He who has begun a good work in you will complete it until the day of Jesus Christ."
–Philippians 1:6

From the cradle to the grave, God is faithful. When we have a sense of God speaking to our hearts, we must listen. We must follow. When we trust Him completely, we can easily give Him the glory for the journey.

APPLICATION

A. Acknowledge that you don't have all the answers. Ask for guidance. Ask for wisdom.
B. Believe that His plan is good. Seeking His will and His way is the best.
C. Claim the promises that are found in the Scriptures. He speaks to us personally. He reveals His desires and His purposes as we seek a relationship with our heavenly Father diligently and daily.

PRAYER

Our loving heavenly Father, as we seek Your wisdom and Your ways, we know that our times are in Your hands. You are aware of every need and every desire of our hearts, and we bring all of these into Your presence.

We submit and surrender our own will to follow Your guidance. We pray for special illumination for the decisions ahead, and we offer praise and thanksgiving for all that You do for us. Help us, Father, to live in Your light. Help us to reflect that light and love in our surroundings so that others may come to know You also. Amen.

Endnotes

[3] Ellen G. White, *The Great Controversy* (Pacific Press Publishing, Revised ed., 2002) 354

Mind, Body, and Spirit

– 12 –

Time and Eternity

WE ARE PHYSICAL, emotional, and spiritual beings. We are fearfully and wonderfully made. Each one of us is a masterpiece. The body itself is an incredible creation. Systems are integrated together, full of life. We have the breath of life. How many years have our hearts kept beating? How many miles have our feet carried us since the day we learned how to walk?

Much research has been done on different types of development—physical, mental, emotional, and spiritual. Our potential and capacity are remarkable. We experience our lives within the limits of time. We've only just begun. This is not the end. We have this hope of eternity placed in our hearts (Ecclesiastes 3:11). This hope overshadows us, encircling us entirely, and not only in time but for eternity. There is within us a capacity for creative imagination that catches a glimpse of glory, of the *forever* that is promised in the Word of God.

    The journey to maturity, to wholeness, is a process. It includes differentiating between right and wrong, good and bad, light and darkness. And we make choices to live in this world. We make choices to survive, to make sense of our existence. We struggle to figure it out and make up rules to go by. To some extent, we succeed in establishing the parameters for our worldview; however, we face the reality that everyone else is working through their own lens of understanding also, and we clash. We disagree. We resist, creating conflict.

    This is where the message of the gospel enters. We see Jesus on the cross. The central focus of all history is the Lamb of God, the Son of God,

Mind, Body, and Spirit

sacrificed on the cruel cross of this world by men who were created by Him. The sin of the whole world has been embraced by a loving God reconciling all things to Himself, defeating the power of darkness and death by His love, mercy, and forgiveness. The sinner-saint becomes the redeemed in Christ, made whole by His life, death, and resurrection. This is the grace and the love of God which took on the evil of the whole world and bore it in His own body for our sake. This is grace, marvelous grace, amazing grace.

We move from dualistic thinking to an inclusive, non-judgemental, non-violent perspective, from which we can live with contradictions. We can accept paradoxes and mysteries without fully understanding them. We are open to others. We don't have to be right. We learn to live and let live. We embrace the darkness by embracing Him, and in doing so, we become changed.

We move from the Ten Commandments of Exodus 20 to the Beatitudes of Matthew 5. Loving acceptance brings wholeness to our being. Jesus said that He came to fulfill the law. There is a progression to maturity in the faith. It is a matter of learning to live in the light of the One who is the light.

REFLECTION

"Come to Me, all you who labour and are heavy laden, and I will give you rest. Take My yoke upon you and learn from Me, for I am gentle and lowly in heart, and you shall find rest for your souls. For My yoke is easy and My burden is light."
—Matthew 11:28

"And I have declared to them Your name, and will declare it, that the love with which You loved Me may be in them, and I in them."
—John 17:26

APPLICATION

A. Acknowledge that life in many ways seems divided, fragmented into parts.

B. Believe that God invites us to a unity of body, mind, and spirit to become whole.

C. Claim His promises, and accept that it is the work of the Holy Spirit to bring about this sacred unity. Trust Him to accomplish it.

PRAYER

Our Father in heaven, You are the Creator of all things. We acknowledge your power and majesty throughout the universe. As Your children, we humbly submit and surrender to Your love and light. We believe that You reveal Yourself to us through nature, through Your Word, and through a close relationship with You by faith. You work in us to bring us to wholeness and unity. Only in Your presence, in Your light, can we learn to live lightly. May it be so. Amen.

Conclusion

EACH OF THE PREVIOUS CHAPTERS has a subtitle that alludes to a division of thought/either-or dualistic thinking. The final chapter focuses on the integration of all aspects of our existence, the both-and perspective, in the embrace of faith in God, our Creator, whose design for us is unity within ourselves, unity with the created order, and unity with the Creator Himself. We are one.

FINAL THOUGHT

> Jesus lifts the souls that turn to Him for refuge above the accusing and the strife of tongues. No man or evil angel can impeach these souls. Christ unites them to His own divine-human nature. They stand beside the great Sin Bearer in the light proceeding from the throne.
>
> —Ellen G. White, *Ministry of Healing*, 28

All praise, honor, and glory be unto Jesus!

About the Author

Jane Holmes is a Christian who has followed the Lord from the time she was ten years old, when she heard and responded to the message about Jesus as Saviour and Lord. She is a retired teacher, a mother of two grown daughters, and Nana to five grandchildren. She is active in the Red Deer Seventh-day Adventist Church and attests to the loving presence and faithfulness of God. She invites readers to enter that journey of faith in order to walk in the light. Writing about this journey is her latest joy in touching others' lives with the light of truth, who is the living Lord.

Follow Jane

Website: healthandhopeministries.ca
Email: mrswtjj2002@gmail.com

FREE survey and initial consultation with Jane on the website.

Health Leaders

Susan Peirce Thompson, brightlineeating.com

Chris Wark, chrisbeatcancer.com

Sandy Grant, Durham School of Health and Nutrition, dshneducate.com

James Colquohoun and Laurentine ten Bosch, foodmatters.com

Jonathon Zita, lifestylecanada.org

John and Ocean Robbins, foodrevolution.org

Charlotte Gerson, gerson.org

Robyn Openshaw, greensmoothiegirl.com

Ty and Charlene Bollinger, thetruthaboutcancer.com

Dr Izabella Wentz, thyroidpharmacist.com

Dr. Neil Nedley, weimar.edu

Can You Help?

Reviews are everything to an author because they mean a book is given more visibility. If you enjoyed this book, please review it on your favourite book review sites and tell your friends about it. Thank you!

Made in the USA
Monee, IL
15 February 2021